David Remfry DANCERS

ESSAYS BY

Edward Lucie-Smith

Dore Ashton

Carter Ratcliff

INTERVIEW WITH THE ARTIST BY

Alanna Heiss

David Remfry

DANCERS

Boca Raton Museum of Art

This catalogue was published
in conjunction with the exhibition
"David Remfry / Dancers,"
originated by:

 BOCA RATON
MUSEUM OF ART

Mizner Park
501 Plaza Real
Boca Raton, FL 33432

Telephone: 561.392.2500
Fax: 561.391.6410
www.bocamuseum.org

Exhibition Curator: George S. Bolge

Exhibition Dates
November 12, 2002 – January 12, 2003

Traveling to the Fitzwilliam Museum,
Cambridge, England, in 2005

Design: Anthony McCall Associates, New York
Editor: Caroline Hansberry
Copyeditor: John Anderson
Printed and bound by Mondadori Printing, Italy

Cover:
DANCERS (detail)
2001
Watercolor on Paper (Two panels)
40 x 100 in.

Page 1:
DANCERS
1985
Graphite on Paper
40½ x 27¼ in.

First published in 2002 by Boca Raton Museum of Art.
Essays © Boca Raton Museum of Art and the authors.

First edition
Printed in Italy

Library of Congress
Cataloging-in-Publication Data
2002106312

Remfry, David, 1942–
    David Remfry / Edward Lucie-Smith / Dore Ashton /
    Carter Ratcliff / Alanna Heiss.
        p. cm.
    Issued in conjunction with an exhibition.
    Includes bibliographical references.
    ISBN 0-936859-42-3 (hardcover : alk. paper)
    ISBN 0-936859-41-5 (softcover : alk. paper)
    1. Remfry, David, 1942---Exhibitions. I. Lucie-Smith, Edward /
Ashton, Dore / Ratcliff, Carter / Heiss, Alanna II. Boca Raton
Museum of Art

This book is made possible through the generous
support of the Avellino Family Foundation, Inc.,
the Gelsomina Foundation, The Charles and Lynn Kramer Family
Foundation, Margaret Lipworth-Becker,
Mutual of America, Heidi Neuhoff, and anonymous sponsors.

MUTUAL OF AMERICA

David Remfry *Dancers*
is a sponsored
project of
NYFA

CONTENTS

ACKNOWLEDGMENTS

The idea for this exhibition and book originated in David Remfry's studio in the Hotel Chelsea, New York in 1999. David showed me a group of pictures he referred to as the Dancers which he had begun to paint in 1985 but had never exhibited before. By 1999, they numbered over 70 pictures. As he brought out painting after painting, I began to envision an exhibition devoted solely to the Dancers. I feel privileged that David has chosen the Boca Raton Museum of Art for the premier exhibition of this important body of work.

Many people made valuable contributions to this exhibition and book. I would like to acknowledge, on behalf of the Boca Raton Museum of Art, the cooperation of the lenders and galleries who have made David Remfry's work available to us. I am extremely grateful to Edward Lucie-Smith, Dore Ashton, and Carter Ratcliff for their insightful essays, and to Alanna Heiss, who kindly allowed us to reproduce her provocative interview with the artist. Caroline Hansberry was indispensable in coordinating the international tour of the exhibition and this book.

I would like to express my gratitude to the Avellino Family Foundation, Inc., the Gelsomina Foundation, The Charles and Lynn Kramer Family Foundation, Margaret Lipworth-Becker,

Mutual of America, Heidi Neuhoff and the New York Foundation for the Arts, and the sponsors who wish to remain anonymous, for their generous support of this exhibition and book. In addition, my sincere appreciation goes out to the following underwriters whose enlightened support helped to subsidize the realization of this worthwhile undertaking: Citigroup Private Bank; Sun-Sentinel; Autohaus-Pompano; Tiffany & Co; Hodgson Russ LLP; American Express Company; Champion Porsche; Premier Estate Properties; Publix Super Markets; Salomon Smith Barney-Citigroup Foundation; Mellon Private Asset Management; Bloomingdale's; and Burdines.

Supplementary funding for our programming is provided by grants from the Florida Department of State, Division of Cultural Affairs, the Florida Arts Council; the Palm Beach County Tourist Development Cultural Activities Fund, and the Palm Beach Cultural Council.

I would like to recognize our institution's Board of Trustees, led by Phyllis Rubin, President, for enabling the Museum to realize its ambitious, diverse, and internationally recognized exhibition program.

Finally, I would like to applaud the unfailing support of my staff, whose daily achievements are a constant source of encouragement.

George S. Bolge
Executive Director,
Boca Raton Museum of Art

The purest painting is the one that refreshes the alphabet of one's eyes: the delicious shock of color, a form that radically redefines. The story or the content will reach the brain in a secondary lapse of time. First comes the aesthetic surprise, the ravishment, which holds every other consideration in sway. It is a rare enough phenomenon, and by all accounts, some people never experience it in painting, which they approach as an enigma to be explained or a sum of knowledge to be absorbed. Yet without that initial thrill on the aesthetic nerve, the painting as painting – like the poem as poetry – does not exist. Memorable images provoke a moment of suspension during which the paint acts at a subconscious level on a sensibility.

We experience a unique, joyous sensation from the work of David Remfry, a sensation rarely felt nowadays in society. By communicating this sensation adroitly through a confluence of colors and forms, he inspires us to discover it within ourselves and to communicate it to others. Remfry does not strive for perfection in the literal sense in his renderings, because he realizes that such a pursuit is superhuman. Each painting offers us expanses of spontaneity, one or two realities which in turn precipitate several other realities. In the same way, but without any realistic systematizing, each color appears as if deriving from the participation of other colors.

There is a magical moment captured during the "dance" that can inspire as much apprehension as joy, and this is the axis upon which this exhibition revolves. His paintings of dancers are a spontaneous, yet fabulously cunning, invitation to set one's sight free. Law and stale habit, all the usual ways of looking, are banished. There are neither maps nor boundaries. The eye makes its own road, confronts its own apparitions, and arrives at the place of its shooting. It crosses continents of kaleidoscopic change to reach a firmament in which the most earthbound fantasy can fly; yet nowhere in the gravity-shorn world does chaos prevail. The proliferating mass of pictorial elements is contained in a hair's-breadth equilibrium.

If one looked for a general definition of Remfry's overall achievement, it might be complexity of detail held in the most delicate and precarious equilibrium. Tonal resonance and the fine balance of parts to the whole became the terrain on which he was to engage his plastic skills. A sense of freedom, even of freewheeling fantasy, prevailed, but somewhere unobtrusively it was kept in check by a subtle discipline that gave authority to the intricate play of scattered pigment. "Play" is the operative word, for Remfry put himself into these compositions with the seriousness of a child at play, something that Nietzsche specifically recommended to artists.

Time and again, the artist rejoices in the very act of seeing, the visual possession and transformation of life. In order to paint, the artist opens the "window" of the paper to the inside and, at the same time, to the outside. He provides us with a cornucopia of sensations, which encourage us to have freedom of thought.

Finally, what strikes one most in this body of work is the long song of praise to sight and its gathering freshness. Innocence, curiosity, and desire haunt Remfry's paintings. The source has widened but never grown tainted. This is the world of a man whom the dreams of childhood have never failed.

G. S. B.

SWING (detail)

DAVID REMFRY

DANCERS

Edward Lucie-Smith

I

IT IS NO SECRET that we live in an age that is obsessed with the idea of innovation. To a
certain extent, this obsession is justified by the speed of technological progress. Until recently, the
perception perhaps was that this could not continue at the rate achieved during the closing years
of the 20th century, but the continuing rapid development of both computer and genetic sciences
now suggests the contrary.

Since the surrounding environment inevitably affects art, there has also been an assumption,
on the part of many critics, and also by artists themselves, that artworks must be drastically modified
in order to play their part in this new technological world. Sometimes this perception is voiced in
extremely crude and simplistic terms. For example, there is the idea, prevalent in a number of recent
major survey exhibitions, that traditional methods of making art are now at their last gasp, and
that only artworks that employ technological methods of image making will do. This has been
carried further, in the official sanction offered to forms of art that are defiantly non-perceptual —
in other words, where the visual element plays little or no part in what they have to offer.

Despite this, a number of contemporary artists have continued to be fascinated with purely
traditional methods of image making. David Remfry is one of these. The paradox is that he, and
other artists somewhat like him, have now, almost in spite of themselves, begun to acquire a revolutionary look. The situation can perhaps be equated with the one that existed in Italy in the
closing years of the 16th century. The Mannerist style had then been triumphant in Italian studios
for more than fifty years. Associated in its early years with a number of very great artists —
among them Michelangelo, Pontormo, Bronzino and Parmigianino — it was, by the 1580s and
1590s, visibly reaching the end of its trajectory. In particular, artistic theory had become
increasingly triumphant, at the expense of artistic practice.

A typical figure of this period was the Milanese-born Giovanni Paolo Lomazzo (1538–1600).
Lomazzo was originally trained as a painter but, after going blind at the age of 33, set himself up
as a theoretician, who in two influential books, one published in 1584 and the other in 1590,
laid down a multitude of rules for artists to follow. His work is conspicuous for its hostility to the
idea that nature is the source of all beauty. In other words, he had something in common with
a number of leading art theorists writing today, who are equally hostile to the idea of art as something modeled on what the artist finds in the world surrounding him.

The paradox is, of course, that the years when Lomazzo was at his most influential were
also those that saw the emergence of Caravaggio, who arrived in Rome somewhere between 1588
and 1592. Some of Caravaggio's early works, such as the severed head of Medusa painted on

Below left: **SITTING WOMAN WITH HER RIGHT LEG BENT**
Egon Schiele (1890–1918)
1917, Watercolor, Gouache and Charcoal on Paper

Below right: **EMILIE FLOGE**
Gustav Klimt (1862–1918)
1902, Oil on Canvas

a tournament shield (c.1590, now in the Uffizi) are typically Mannerist in their reliance on artifice and trickery. Yet in looking at them one senses that Caravaggio's use of radical naturalism in these works, and yet more so in other, slightly later compositions such as *The Card Players* (Kimbell Museum, Fort Worth) and *The Fortune Teller* (Louvre, both painted in the mid-1590s), is in a certain sense Mannerism's last throw. In Caravaggio's day, to paint in a naturalistic way, from direct observation, was in fact the most shocking and controversial thing a painter could do. Italian Mannerism had, from its beginnings, relied on paradoxical and shocking effects, as much contemporary art tends to do today. Having exhausted all the other resources open to them, naturalism was perhaps the only way that a new generation of painters, with Caravaggio at their head, could hope to make an impact.

II

I am not, however, going to claim that David Remfry is intentionally revolutionary, in the sense that Caravaggio was in the last decade of the

16th century. Remfry is a mid-career artist, who has pursued a strongly independent line throughout his career, first in his native England, later in the United States, where he has chosen to live and work. It is recent events in the American art world that have tended to pull his work towards the center, rather than any conscious desire to bring about change. For example, his most recent exhibition, before the present one, was held at New York's P.S.1 – a gallery that has long been a focus for innovation, and which is usually associated with art in new technological forms. At first sight, his presence there was extremely paradoxical, and yet the work itself seemed quite at home.

Despite Remfry's independence, it is possible to find a considerable amount of background material that relates to his work. It is in fact one of his great strengths that he is firmly rooted in established artistic tradition. This tradition can be looked at from several points of view. For example, if one wants to place him in a broad European context, then the two places one has to look first are the Vienna Secession in pre-World War I Austria, and the Neue Sachlichkeit in Weimar Republic Germany. Egon Schiele (1890–1918) ranks as one of the greatest 20th century draughtsmen, and his older colleague Gustav Klimt (1862–1918), the acknowledged leader of the Secession, is only a little behind him. The thing that makes their drawings special – much more so, in my opinion, than the paintings both of them produced – is the spin they put on the academic tradition they inherited from their 19th century predecessors, such as Hans Makart. Their drawings have a subtle angularity that is different from the somewhat more exaggerated rhythms which one discovers in the work of their near-contemporary Aubrey Beardsley. Beardsley's whiplash line, so influential all over Europe, keeps his figures safely in a frozen world. He is 'decadent,' yes, but it is a decadence that doesn't threaten even when he occasionally makes portraits of his contemporaries, such as the celebrated French actress Réjane.

Schiele, in particular, is very different. We really believe in the existence of the people he depicts. His delinquent adolescents, and, later, during World War I, his portraits of Austrian army officers and Russian prisoners of war, have a profound humanity. When, as so often in his prewar drawings of nudes, he stresses the sexuality of his

models, this has a much more disturbing effect than that made by drawings by Beardsley which are much more overtly erotic. Remfry's subjects come from a part of contemporary society that is maturer and considerably less louche than that which produced Schiele's delinquents, but his depictions are nevertheless full of personality.

The edge he gives them may remind certain viewers of the work of members of a slightly later generation of Germanic artists—those who are now grouped together as members of the Neue Sachlichkeit, and especially, perhaps, of the work of Otto Dix. Certainly Remfry's use of line has some of Dix's characteristic incisiveness. He is also an admirer of the work of Max Beckmann. However, in 20th century German art this quality of incisive observation is linked to sardonic bitterness about the condition of German society under the Weimar Republic—a society with its illusions, as well as its actual economy, shattered by catastrophic defeat. I don't think one senses this apocalyptic mood in Remfry's work. No one could ever see him, for example, as a prophet of the events of 9/11 2001, even though he lives only a few miles from the location of the World Trade Center, and could actually see the catastrophe as it developed from the windows of his apartment.

There is one artist of the inter-war period, rooted not in Germany but in New York itself, whom he does resemble. This is Reginald Marsh (1898–1954). Marsh was a contemporary of, and in some respects is related to, American Regionalists such as Thomas Hart Benton. Nevertheless, there is a big difference. Whereas Benton and his peers celebrated the great American hinterland, Marsh's

subject matter was provided by the place they most hated—the great metropolis of New York. Marsh was particularly interested in the recreational activities of New Yorkers. He shows them on the beaches and boardwalks of Coney Island. He depicts New York street scenes. He has a particular penchant for theater and dance hall scenes, like the example illustrated here. Here again, however, one notes a difference between Remfry's work and the comparison proposed. Marsh's figures tend to be types rather than fully developed portraits of individuals. This characteristic is emphasized by the fact that he suffers from 'horror vacui.' Every part of a Marsh composition is crammed with incident or, if not with actual activity, then with swarming details of all kinds. His New York is a kind of beehive or ant heap, whose inhabitants possess only a purely collective identity.

This difference is perhaps overridden by a more important resemblance. Both Remfry and Marsh are quintessentially urban artists. Though Remfry's subjects emerge as individuals—it is indeed their quirky individuality that seems to supply a large part of the impulse to paint them—they are nevertheless at least partly defined by their context, and that context is never rural or even suburban. They may dress up as cowboys, or at any rate affect a cowboy shirt or hat, but they are clearly not at home on the range.

III

Though the comparisons I have so far chosen to make are all with artists who are not British, it is important to remember that Remfry was born in Britain and spent the first part of his career there. His British roots run deep. While I was in the midst of writing this essay, there came into my hands a sale catalogue of items from the collection of the Marquess of Bath at Longleat. Longleat is one of the greatest of English country houses and its collections have enormous depth—so much so that items can remain hidden and unconsidered for a century and more. Among the things which emerged into the light of day thanks to this dispersal was a till-then-unknown series of drawings and watercolors by Thomas Rowlandson (1756–1827). Rowlandson ranks among the great practitioners of the art of watercolor painting, a form of art that is often seen as quintessentially British. He is unusual among his peers because he put more emphasis on the human figure than he did on landscape. The Longleat watercolors were mostly concerned with a trip Rowlandson made, in the company of his brother-in-law and fellow-artist Samuel Howitt, to the Isle of Wight. They are thus quite a long way from Remfry's typical range of subject matter. However, seeing these hitherto unknown drawings also served to trigger my recollection of more familiar works by Rowlandson – drawings that show London theaters and other places of urban amusement, such as Vauxhall Gardens. In these, Rowlandson not only catches the essence of city life, but he also depicts scores of immediately recognizable individuals, with an economy of line that has ensured his posthumous reputation.

Art historians nevertheless sometimes have difficulty in dealing with Rowlandson's oeuvre. They don't know whether they should categorize him as a caricaturist, like his contemporary James Gillray (1757–1815), or as a peer of the landscape watercolorist Thomas Girtin (1775–1802). In fact, while some of Rowlandson's drawings, and the prints made after them, do rank as caricatures, he never has the edge and bite of Gillray. He is not enraged by human folly and human corruption, as Gillray seems to be; he is simply amused by the quirks of human appearance and human behavior. One could even say that he is quintessentially the poet of the imperfect, rather than the perfect body. In other words, he clearly prefers the too fat or too thin to what is just right – handsome men and very pretty girls tend to be his least successful subjects.

It would be stretching a point to describe Remfry as a caricaturist, even in the very modified and qualified way that Rowlandson is a maker of caricatures. There nevertheless lurks within his work an element of the caricature tradition. It is worth trying to specify what this is. Essentially the thing we now call caricature combines two very different and often antagonistic impulses. One is that of creating allegorical drawings, usually but not always with satirical intent. A good example is the early 16th century woodcut that shows the devil playing Luther as if he were a pair of bagpipes. Luther's plump, double-chinned head becomes the bag that gives the instrument its name. Combinations of this sort anticipate 20th century Surrealism, and Remfry is emphatically not a Surrealist.

Another part of the caricature tradition is specifically related to the art of portraiture, and is more recent in origin. In the last decade of the 16th century, Annibale Carracci (1560–1609), Caravaggio's contemporary and rival in Rome, began making scribbled drawings for his own amusement and that of his immediate circle. These were 'charged' or deliberately exaggerated portraits of the people around him. Instead of suppressing or modifying quirks of appearance – a large nose, a long chin – he exaggerated them. These drawings owed something to the drawings of grotesques previously made by Leonardo da Vinci at the beginning of the 16th century, but whereas Leonardo had rather coldly concerned himself with depicting types that illustrated aspects of Renaissance physiognomic theory, Annibale Carracci wanted to produce an immediately recognizable likeness that would amuse through its evident veracity in the very midst of genial exaggeration. He was so successful in his attempt that the fashion for 'personal' caricatures immediately spread throughout Europe, and continues to flourish today in our own newspapers.

Caricature is generally associated with observation of facial features, but in fact the good caricaturist takes all aspects of the body into account. He or she knows that it is gestures and posture that convey a likeness, even more efficiently than accurate observation of eyes and nose and mouth. This is one of Remfry's great artistic strengths, and one can see from the way he builds up his compositions, sometimes using photographs as reference material, how concerned he is with getting these elements right. He also makes preliminary studies which focus on one element in the composition – for instance, a single pair of dancers excerpted from a larger, frieze-like composition – in order to make certain that his observation is as finely tuned as possible.

IV

These friezes are Remfry's major achievements, and it is worth thinking about the way in which they combine apparently contradictory elements. When we speak of a frieze we are inevitably thinking in 'classical' terms – classical in the purely historical as well as the stylistic sense. The great exemplars of the frieze are, after all, the slabs depicting a procession of worshipers taken from the Parthenon and now in the British Museum. The Parthenon frieze is the benchmark against which all later attempts

SWING
1998
Photographs and Wash
Each photograph 6 x 4 in.

have had to measure themselves. In the late 18th and early 19th centuries many compositions of this sort were created under the auspices of the Europe-wide Neoclassical movement, for example by the British sculptor and draughtsman John Flaxman (1755–1826).

Frieze compositions survived the advent of Modernism in the 20th century. One of the most celebrated of all early Modernist paintings, Matisse's *La Danse*, can in fact be described as a modified frieze—the composition is lateral, but suggests circular motion.

A characteristic of these friezes, both classical, Neoclassical and Modernist, is that they reduce the importance of individual participants, in favor of achieving a unified rhythm for the whole. Thus, for instance, the beautiful nude youths in the Parthenon frieze are clones—apart from shifts in posture, and the attributes they may or may not carry, there is in fact no way of distinguishing one participant in the great procession from the next. Matisse's dancers come close to being face-less robots. The problem Remfry has set himself is how to create convincingly unified friezes which are nevertheless made up of immediately recogniz-able portraits—portraits which, as I have already suggested, are by no means subdued or toned down in the interests of the whole.

In attempting this, he has given himself one important advantage, and that is the overall subject—the idea of dancers and dancing. It is no accident that so many frieze compositions in the past have depicted dancers. Dancing implies a rhythmic progression from one place to another, and this, in a slightly different sense, is what friezes in art are about. They aim to carry the eye along a surface, rather than to encourage the gaze to penetrate within it. Most formal dances consist of stylized, repetitive movements. The fact that this precise repetition of movements and gestures is 'against nature' is one of the things, perhaps the chief thing, that seems to turn dance into a genuine form of artistic expression.

Yet of course contemporary social dancing is no longer like this. It consists of a multitude of free gestures and movements, born of the impulse of the moment. In Remfry's large watercolor *Swing* (p. 70), for example, we see four couples, a partial view of another couple (a woman whose partner is concealed), and, at the far right, a single female

figure. The couples are holding one another, but there is no uniformity about the way they relate. One woman leans back against her partner's right forearm; one gestures ecstatically while her partner holds her by the waist; the central couple adopt a more traditional pose, hands interlaced; the man who forms one half of the couple at the right leans against and is supported by his female partner. Meanwhile, the woman to the extreme right seems to dance completely on her own, though she may have a partner out of sight, who is cropped by the edge of the composition. What an expert on contemporary social dance might perceive in this is a remnant of more formal patterns, eroded both by the new freedom and an increasing lack of technique.

Remfry has set himself the task of binding all these spontaneous movements together, to create a rhythmic whole. In fact, as one immediately sees, the unpredictable patterns of modern social dancing are something he has learned to use to his advantage. There is indeed a compositional pattern, a wave-like flow of forms and gestures that reads from left to right — note, for example, the insistent diagonals created in the top half of the first two panels by the dancers' arms. Note, too, the syncopation created by the fact that in the central panel, the man's elbow is cropped, which implies the existence of more space between him and the pair on the right than the composition actually allows. Reference to the studies made for the work shows that this right-hand couple could have adopted a completely different pose. What seems to have prompted the change was the need to reveal the single figure clad in red, which now provides such a firm conclusion to the wave-like progression of forms I have described.

Rhythm is never the Remfry's sole preoccupation, however. He is concerned with the way people relate to one another — the emotional overtones of the dance encounter — and also with the social context. As he said in a recent interview with Alanna Heiss, director of P.S.1 in New York: "I'm fascinated by the human predicament. I'm obsessed with people, with us, how we behave together. The things that link us, what we do together, what we do after hours, after a drink or two at clubs, at bars and at parties. How we embrace as we dance, how we 'distract ourselves' as Francis Bacon put it. I love observing all this

and recording it in a painting. In the process, I hope to discover something of what we are."

It is noticeable that a number of his paintings show female couples dancing together. This subject has its own history in art — for example, there are the lesbian couples shown dancing together in some of Toulouse-Lautrec's paintings of the Moulin Rouge. Interestingly enough, in Remfry's work there is no lesbian implication, even in the occasional painting that makes direct reference to turn-of-the-century models. One painting of two young women in long blue-grey dresses can be referred fairly directly to images by Gustav Klimt, for instance. Remfry's girls are not dancing to express sexual attraction, but because they enjoy the activity, and also, perhaps, because they can't persuade the boys to join them. One especially charming painting, *A Little Night Music* (p. 99), shows four girls, each apparently dancing alone, each happy to give herself up to the music. They are obviously not professional dancers. The pair facing the spectator don't have dancers' bodies — they are both a little heavy. The one on the left glances sideways at her companion and kicks one leg backward. It seems as if she is only just beginning to join in, while the woman beside her is already fully possessed by the rhythm, holding up both hands and snapping her fingers in time as she moves.

Remfry's paintings are full of psychological observations of this kind — observations about relationships, and about the characters of his subjects. This is not surprising, as the models are often people he knows well. When he was still working in London, for example, he would ask friends to come and dance in his studio. The earliest couple were two Germans, Claudia Blume and Uve Schalm. He would put some music on; they would dance; he would make sketches. Soon after this, another couple, Victor Arwas and Gretha Hamer, began to work with him in the same way. Victor is a large, bulky man who is an expert in Art Nouveau and Art Deco objects. The music Remfry chose was tangos, even though the couple concerned didn't really know how to tango correctly. Their relationship developed as they danced. Remfry recollects that one picture of them was made on the very day they decided to get married. The strange thing, however, was that the sketches made at these sessions were not made with any particular end in view – for a planned exhibition, for instance. For the time being Remfry simply put them aside. The series only began in 1985/6, and even then the artist didn't realize that the theme would become the subject for a series.

Long before this, however, he remembers being interested in dance and in popular entertainment. He recalls some of his earliest reactions, which go back to 1959:

> In Hull on the east coast of England, flanked by the River Humber and buffeted by the bitter winds of the North Sea, I was raised in this great seaport and it was there that the germ of my affection for dance and dancers grew, more as a voyeur because I loved to observe and draw.
>
> It was in the late fifties, and rock and roll was born. Teddy boys and floppy-suited fisher boys were gods. Girls squeezed into tight sweaters revealing un-life-like conical breasts, concentric rings and all, and layers and layers of petticoats which mushroomed out as they twirled on the dance floor, all topped by cotton-candy, teased and back-combed hair and dabbed liberally with Evening in Paris. This was when I learned of the exciting and bad things to be done away from your parents. I was scared and thrilled by the dancers at the dubious youth clubs and at the Locarno, and City Hall. The Teddy boys carried razors or flick knives, and fights were frequent and vicious.
>
> One night at the Locarno, the music was playing and there was a flurry in the middle of the dance floor, a muted scream, and a man sagged to the floor, stabbed and bleeding. As he was carried out and the assailant pinioned and led away, the music resumed, barely a few bars gap, and the dancing continued as though nothing had happened. I watched the blood travel like a macabre dance diagram, on the soles of oblivious dancers.

After leaving art school, Remfry moved to London. He lived in Earls Court, which was then and still is an area for pub and club entertainment. Here he became fascinated with the Ronettes – three Hispanic women, with beehive hair-dos, who formed part of an early 1960's rock and roll group dreamt up by Phil Specter – his wife Ronnie Specter was the lead singer. Remfry says now: "(The Ronettes) performed and Remfry went along. He sketched, bought their records, went home and painted them, trying to incorporate a feeling of their movement. The series continued for two or three years."

From this it was a gradual transition to more elaborate paintings of dancers. Some of the earliest – they date from 1985 – were inspired by visits to the dances held at Hammersmith Town Hall in London:

> I started hanging out at the afternoon tea dances, to observe and draw. For 50p, (75c) you got a cup of tea and a biscuit, and the opportunity to dance all afternoon to big band records.
>
> This drew an older age group – Senior Citizens mostly. I liked the mix of flashy dancers – ones who knew what they were doing, and others who could barely walk, but who would somehow get up and dance. There was a lack of men and it was quite common to see two women dancing together.

Later still, in New York, around 1983, Remfry used to go to the famous Roseland dance hall, which he had already heard about in England. "It was a legend. They had a live band that played ballroom standards, foxtrots, waltzes and Latin at intervals. The difference between here and Hammersmith was that they could almost all dance well at Roseland – the competition was much stronger!" He has stories to tell about the experience, some sad, some comic, some both at once:

> I was sitting at a table in Roseland, surreptitiously drawing dancers. A couple befriended me and every so often would come back to the table, like swimmers who urge dry poolside softies to come in and enjoy the water. I had been watching a man dancing by himself. Women do this all the time. A woman will put her handbag in the dance floor and dance around it and not seem out of place. But the man was different, he had a transfixed stare and a sort of half smile, his arm curved around a waist that wasn't there: his hand clasped only air. I asked my new friends, Sally and Jack, who was the man and what was he doing?
>
> "Oh that's Al," Jack told me. "His wife died six weeks ago." It then became a less

IZZY ORT'S
Edward Burra (1905–1976)
1955, Watercolor and Pencil on Paper

STUDY FOR ALL NIGHT LONG
Michael Andrews (1928–1995)
1964, Oil on Canvas

amusing and more poignant scene to me and
I said, "How sad!" "That ain't sad," retorted
Sally in a withering New Jersey cadence. "He
cheated on her for 40 years."

V

If the Dancers series is the product of an obsessive
interest both in the subject itself and in human
relationships in general, it can also be located
in the recent history of British art—and I think it
is fair to say that, though both his residence and
his subject matter are now American, Remfry still
remains in some ways a very British artist. He
notes, for example, that the first work representing
dancers that attracted him was a reproduction
of a painting by the Bloomsbury artist Roger Fry
(1866–1934), which he saw when he was still
an art student. He remembers that, while he didn't
especially like the painting itself, he found the
subject really interesting, and that he asked the
life model who worked for the school, one Miss
Garnier, to hold her arms out in the pose of the
Fry picture, and in this way did his own version.

The British artists who have directly influenced
him are mostly members of the so-called 'School
of London,' a catch-all term invented by the
American painter R.B. Kitaj, who was for a long
time a London resident. Remfry is an admirer
of Francis Bacon, and in particular of Bacon's fluid
dexterity in using paint. However, the School of
London painter he most closely resembles, both in
technical approach and in subject-matter, is the
late Michael Andrews (1928–1995), who is considerably less known in the United States. Andrews

shared with Remfry a fascination with clubs and
nocturnal entertainment. He also shared Remfry's
oscillation between extremely fluid handling and
a photographic approach to representing the figure
—photographic in the sense that these figures
are shown in the poses familiar from snapshots,
momentary in the true sense that no model in
the studio could hope to hold them for long.
Andrews, like Remfry, was fascinated by twilight
zones—social twilight zones, rather than purely
painterly ones. Another School of London painter
who has from time to time ventured into this
area is of course Lucian Freud.

Another British artist who immediately springs
to mind when one looks at Remfry's work is
Edward Burra (1905–1976) who is, like Stanley
Spencer, one of the great unclassifiables of 20th
century British art. There are two quite different
reasons for this. One is that Remfry and Burra
treat similar subject matter. *Izzy Ort's*, illustrated
here, is typical of a certain period in Burra's artistic activity. Burra's passion for what is sometimes
called 'low life' is a conspicuous feature of the
early part of his career. Yet there are differences.
Izzy Ort's is in fact an American subject—a blue-
collar bar in Boston. For Burra, a fragile homosex-
ual Englishman from a wealthy family, a milieu
of this kind was something truly exotic. His letters

on this and kindred subjects often read like excerpts from Ronald Firbank's high camp novella *Valmouth*. Though Burra's subject matter is sometimes close to Remfry's, the whole emotional tone of their work is in fact very different. The second reason for putting the two artists together is more concrete. Both make use of watercolor on a large scale. As I have already said, when speaking of certain resemblances between Remfry and Thomas Rowlandson, watercolor is often regarded as a quintessentially British medium. However, watercolor work on a very large scale remains rare, both in Britain and elsewhere.

Both Burra and Remfry originally adopted watercolor, in preference to oils for reasons of health. They enlarged the scale of their work because they wanted it to have the kind of impact associated with the rival method of painting. Burra was a semi-invalid throughout his life. Remfry, in 1979, was struck down by a serious illness that attacked both his respiratory system and his joints. When he started to recover, he still felt very weak. Oil painting was physically too strenuous, so when he went back to work he started making small watercolors. Meanwhile a Los Angeles dealer saw and liked some drawings he had made previously and left with a friend in New York. In complete ignorance of his condition, she rang and offered him a show. Remfry accepted, and set to work – using watercolor, to which he had now become accustomed. As he says now: "The new paintings became a celebration of my recovery." A very successful celebration, as the show sold out. The watercolors he made then, however, were mostly single figures and still lifes, though there were also occasional images of dancers practicing at ballet school. The perfection of ballet-trained bodies, however, gave him the feeling that the images still lacked something. It was only gradually that he discovered a way to combine his fascination with the idea of dance – ordinary people dancing – with his formidable new range of technical skills.

In Remfry's paintings of Dancers one sees how imperfect human beings – imperfect physically, and also no doubt in character – aspire towards an idea of perfection. Caught up in the movements of the dance, they exist, momentarily, in a different sphere from the one they normally inhabit.

The images in the series remind me of some verses from 'Orchestra', a great but too little known poem by the Elizabethan writer Sir John Davies (1569–1626):

Behold the world, how it is whirlèd round
    And for it is so whirl'd is namèd so;
In whose large volume many rules are found
    Of this new art, which it doth fairly show.
    For your quick eyes in wandering to and fro,
        From east to west, on no one thing can glance,
        But, if you mark it well, it seems to dance.

Only the earth doth stand forever still:
    Her rocks remove not, nor her mountains meet,
Although some wits enriched with learning's skill
    Say heaven stands firm and that the earth doth fleet,
    And swiftly turneth underneath their feet;
        Yet, though the earth is ever steadfast seen,
        On her broad breast has dancing ever been.

Edward Lucie-Smith and David Remfry at the Hotel Chelsea, January 17, 2002

O BODY SWAYED TO MUSIC (detail)

THE DANCE

Dore Ashton

THE WORD "CHARACTER" is too often used rather cavalierly. It loses the sharpness of its origins. In the beginning, character was a thing; a tool for incising, an instrument for marking. It bore the pressure of the hand. It sought, guided by a sure hand, to burrow inward. I think David Remfry's work carries in itself the keen spirit of the word's origins. His desire to render the precise character of the dance as it animates its human performers can be felt throughout his work. Remfry extends an ancient tradition: In his characterization of a single dancer; two dancers; a throng of dancers, he is characterizing a milieu, an urban life, a specific epoch and a timeless time all at once. He does with shapes and form what Aristotle's protégé Theophrastus did with words in the third century B.C. In a book titled *Characters*, Athens with all its velleities springs to life through individual characters whose distinctive traits Theophrastus delineated with a piercing eye and considerable humor.

Among other things, Remfry is a connoisseur of dancehalls and their denizens. When he first visited New York in 1978, he quickly discovered our premier dancehall, Roseland—a place I happen to know well. For years I watched and danced there. I came to understand that Roseland was the only classless society I would ever know. There, no matter how lowly your daily life, if you were an elegant dancer you were an aristocrat. Dishwashers and janitors became princes, and elderly retired chorus girls, princesses. Not only that, but the youthful princes often selected the elderly princesses solely on the basis of their superior aptitudes on the dance floor. This leveling of classes abets Remfry's natural benevolence as an observer. He registers them all with affection, and sometimes with humor, and imaginatively determines their specific characteristics, respecting, always, the one among the many. I don't mean to say that Remfry's foraging is limited to dancehalls. His extreme attention to the circumstances of the dance is extended to parties and night clubs and even to the streets. Often he persuades dancers to enter his studio and dance. They are from many walks of life, ranging from the owner of the colorful Hotel Chelsea, where Remfry lives and works, to uptown businessmen, to young women he has spotted at parties.

I see Remfry's undertaking as the characterization not so much of dancers as of something more abstract: the dance. That is because Remfry is no mere academic tracing the outlines of a model. He belongs to a larger tradition. Perhaps to the enthralled literature of the later 19th century which insisted you could not tell the dancer from the dance. This reaching for the larger abstraction lifts Remfry's work from the realm of the topical illustrator. Pausing over his works, I thought of the larger thoughts that the dance has inspired in such poets as Mallarmé and his admirer Paul Valéry, who lent his poet's eye—trained by the great master, Degas—to the dance:

And as thought, when excited, touches every substance,
oscillates between pauses and instants, overleaps all
differences; and as hypotheses are symmetrically formed
in our mind, and as possibilities are arranged
and numbered—so this body exercises itself in
all its parts, combines with itself, takes on
shape after shape, and continuously leaves itself!...
Its acts are no longer distinguishable from its limbs....

Much of Remfry's work does, as Valéry puts it,
oscillate between pauses and instants. His compositions—for like every true painter, he is obliged
to compose—are at once fluent and static. He is
well aware that the body exercises itself in all its
parts in the dance, but that certain parts carry
more explicitly expressive intentions. It is not just
swaying, dipping, charging, or languorously inclin-
ing generality he is after. He intones. The music
that induces these movements demands explicit-
ness that is to be found most readily in the
extremities. It is often in the balletic composition
of shoes, or the disposition of hands that the
abstraction, the dance, is embodied in his work.

It is obvious that, as Kleist so eloquently
wrote, all dancers, like all marionettes, perform
from a center of gravity which governs even
the movement of extremities. I imagine that Remfry
seizes first the single most expressive line of the
body as it moves from the invisible central axis.
But then, he must characterize both dancer and
dance through gesture. We often talk rather glibly
of body language. Nowhere does that language
find its inherent grammar more than in the dance.
Hands and feet are verbs. Notice with what care
Remfry describes the position of hands. The soli-
tary dancer may seek equilibrium by splaying
her hands wide, or seek the singular still moment
by dropping the hands low upon her thighs.
The duo, obliged to become one in the dance, is
dependent on the placement of hands. Remfry
always notices how firmly or how gingerly, how
gracefully or how awkwardly the one grasps the
other (not to mention *where* the hands grasp, an
occasion for Remfry's gentle humor). He notices
also how immensely varied social relations and
mores of the dance floor can be. Without intending it, Remfry functions as a sociologist and even
a diagnostician. That couple with its voracious-
seeming female may well be mismatched. Or that
couple with no space between them, suit and
dress the same hue, may find themselves in
harmony only on the dance floor. One is always
tempted to guess life stories in Remfry's work
and to wonder who those entwined figures may
really be. Riddles. Another painter I knew,
Philip Guston, relished such riddles and recited
to me an old English nursery rhyme with the
refrain "If this be not I, who then may it be?"

There is a book title by a wonderful writer,
Guy Davenport, that condenses a large truth in
five words: "Every force evolves a form." There
are forces behind Remfry's paintings. They range
from cultural memory (such as the peculiar way
Bacon used platforms in his paintings) to material
substances and their histories. He paints with
watercolor. The medium itself has a history that
I'm sure he has ingested. Not only the 19th-century
Norwich school of his native England where he
trained, but Goya, Delacroix, Grosz, Picasso and
so many others might figure in the forces that
helped to evolve the forms in Remfry's work.

The particularities of watercolor include its
transparency, washes and propensity for utilizing
the light of its paper ground. Watercolor also
works very well with the refinements of pencil lines.
Once having noted that these are watercolors,

I will agree with the painter that they are in fact
paintings and not the dainty small offerings of
members of watercolor societies. Remfry works
large. The ultimate forces that evolve his forms are
born within the paintings and from his painter's
culture. And they can be quite complex. Some com-
mentators have noted his tendency to crop, seeing
in it influences from film and video. But after all,
there was Degas. We know he cropped his compositions in order to stress the thrust of his dancers,
and to suggest the way they modified the studio
spaces in which they practiced, or the stages on
which they performed. Cropping tends to bring the
figure forward, close to the picture plane—a formal
approach developed when modern artists conceived
space laterally and renounced vanishing-point per-
spective. Remfry, I think, instinctively holds to the
planar vision, often working with diagonal planes to
suggest near and not-near. The idiom is modern.

The tendency inherent in the modern tradition
is most evident when Remfry brings together more
than one dancer in carefully studied attitudes. Quite
often he composes diptychs or triptychs in which,
through a kind of rhyming of forms, or colors, he
harkens to what is outside the painting—the rhythms
of the music to which the dancers respond. Accents
are in the details such as a red dancing slipper, a
striking hat, a swirl of a gauzy skirt. Since Remfry's
figures are observed but not mechanically recorded,
they breathe in couplings and disjunctions over
the entire picture plane. Sometimes a characteristic
gesture recurs in entirely different circumstances,
such as a dancer hitching up her voluminous skirt
in *A Little Night Music*, 1994 (p. 99), in which
Remfry works with large and theatrical volumes
and ambiguous spaces, and the diptych *O Body
Swayed to Music*, 1999 (p. 98), in which the slender
figures read across like notes on a score and con-
clude with the cropped figure at the right turned
away from us. Although both compositions are
figured with women in black, and both are com-
posed of a similar palette of black, ochre and flesh
tones, Remfry creates totally different configura-
tions, and above all, different moods.

Dancers they are, these shapes that Remfry
draws so effortlessly, but by the natural extension of
the imagination, they are also the dance, a primary
abstraction created through millennia and renewed
by each generation's artists, among whom Remfry
is exemplary.

DANCERS (detail)

DAVID REMFRY

The Meaning of the Dance,
the Dance of Meaning

Carter Ratcliff

SOME ART IS MADE FOR CRITICISM. On a silver platter it hands me nicely packaged issues — appropriation or modularity or something grand like abstraction or the sublime. David Remfry's art isn't like that. Instead of issues to examine, he gives me situations to deal with as best I can. Frankly, the denizens of some of his scenes look a bit too hip for me. I don't get all the cues. A tattoo in the small of a young woman's back, for example, always bewilders me, and whatever explanation I'm given usually leaves me feeling even more out of it than before. Remfry, who was born in 1942, doesn't have this sort of problem. Among the young and the old, the thin and the portly, the hip and the unhip, he is at home. I have the feeling that all his subjects in all their variety like to pose for him — rather, they like the way he encourages them to move, to dance, to get wrapped up in themselves and one another. Playing no favorites and yet never detached, he gives each dancer the same degree of attention, at once intense and tactful. There is an amazing fluidity to his attentiveness, and it carries over to his brushwork.

Nearly always, Remfry paints with watercolors. This is a delicate medium. You could say that it is *the* delicate medium, the one that signals a painter's refinement or at least the hope of it. Remfry is an extremely refined artist, but not in any familiar manner. His originality begins with the new uses he has found for his favored medium. Most paintings in watercolor are small. Remfry's are large, sometimes remarkably so. Among his more expansive works are frieze-like pictures forty inches high and one hundred inches wide. Thus he raises watercolor to a monumental scale, and the effect is quietly shocking.

I'm not suggesting that no other artist has ever made big watercolor paintings. Remfry's English background includes any number of late eighteenth- and early nineteenth-century artists — the best known is J. M. W. Turner — who covered sizeable sheets of paper with floods of watercolor. Yet I don't see these artists as Remfry's direct ancestors, for they were landscape painters, and their colors flowed on the currents of the Romantic yearning for unity with Nature. Remfry's subjects are urban, and far from inviting him to feel at one with them, they present him with intractably distinct individualities. Nature with a capital "N" literally never impinges.

To be urban is to be self-consciously civilized. This isn't always easy, for it requires one not only to make peace with the facts of city life but to accept, as well, the fictions of manners and fashion. I call these things fictions because they are contingent, shifting, and in constant need of being reinvented. Yet when we are together, intending to be seen at our civilized best, we act as if they were unquestionable realities — absolutes, of a sort. Thus a certain theatricality tinges the very idea of the metropolis, and we see that drama being played out in every nuance of Remfry's art.

Remfry seems to have entered into an implicit contract with his subjects: they display themselves to him, as openly as they wish, in the expectation that he will transpose their presences, no matter how opaque, into socially negotiable images; thus mutual benefits ensue, as individuality is celebrated in a public way, and the great generality known as society is inflected by the particularities – the quirks and characteristics – of the large and endlessly interesting population we meet in Remfry's pictures. It's as if he paints to remind society of its only legitimate justification, which is to foster the well-being of its members not merely as social units but as distinct and recognizable people. That is a critic's view of his motives. Remfry sees them differently.

Last year, he told Alanna Heiss, the director of P.S. 1 Contemporary Art Center in New York, that he paints because he is "fascinated by the human predicament. I'm obsessed with people, with us, how we behave together. The things that link us, what we do together . . . How we embrace as we dance . . . I love observing all this and recording 'it' in a painting." Entering the give and take of social interaction, he finds his way directly to all that "the human predicament" puts at stake at every moment: our very selves, which is to say, everything people mean, to themselves and to others.

That sort of meaning is constantly in flux. To immerse himself in it as receptively as he does, Remfry needs a tirelessly fluid sensibility. Or, to get back to the studio, his sensibility needs the most fluid medium it can find. Hence watercolor, and the grand ambition that prompts him to use it at a scale usually reserved for oil paint. Among contemporary figure painters, only a few others make large watercolors – Red Grooms and Philip Pearlstein, for example. The contrast with Remfry is instructive.

No matter how crowded, Remfry's compositions always allow us to see – or to surmise – enough to make the full acquaintance of everyone on view. Pearlstein and Grooms do the opposite, each in his own way. Cropping and crowding their subjects, they undermine the separation of figure and ground, often to the point where something like an all-over field appears. All-overness developed in the abstract paintings of Jackson Pollock, Clyfford Still, and several others as they tried to find a pictorial equivalent of the wide-open spaces –

Nature in the New World. And there is an aspiration to Nature, to pre-social truths about people and things, in the compacted images of Pearlstein and Grooms, even when their subjects are obviously city dwellers. The contrast with Remfry is instructive because it is so complete. He never resists for a moment the urbanity of the people he depicts.

In his brighter pictures, faces are splashed with harsh city light, and the characteristic brilliance of his medium persists even in the dim interiors of bars and dance clubs. There is a dark luminosity to those washes of gray or shadowy lavender that let the white of the underlying paper shine through. His opaque black forms have a kind of glow, as well. I'm not sure how that could be, though I think it must have to do with texture. When his black watercolor becomes dense, it turns velvety – not luminous in literal fact, but lush, nonetheless, with all the light it absorbs. You see this effect in fabrics, in hair, even in eyebrows.

The play of tone – of specific qualities of light on the endless variety of skin – blends with expression and gesture to make Remfry's people vividly available to our gaze. Their availability to one another runs the gamut from total to not at all. Some of his dancing couples appear to be in love or, anyway, willing to believe it for the moment. Others hardly seem to know each other. Sometimes, two figures thrown together in an overpopulated club seem to be living on different planets. Yet even then there is a question of attraction: Is it happening or not? The question is, of course, routine. By stressing sexuality no more or less than the manners and mannerisms of his subjects, Remfry encourages desire to permeate his pictures and mix with the optimism and the anxiety that sustain the rituals of public behavior.

Manners can be ironic. Likewise, sexuality can be ambiguous. It is sometimes impossible to tell if a dancer is gay or straight, but not because Remfry is evasive. He pictures precisely what the shared zones of society allow us to see: cues that often admit of no definite reading. Remfry is a realist here, not so much content with appearances as ready and willing to acknowledge that there is nothing else for him to depict. Expressionists, Surrealists, and their many siblings and cousins in the ranks of twentieth-century modernism often claimed to see past appearances to inner truths – to realities with a capital "R." These days, claims

DANCERS (study)
Undated
Watercolor on Paper
5½ x 3¾ in.

DANCERS (study)
Undated
Watercolor on Paper
5½ x 3¾ in.

of that sort sound like so much metaphysical pretension. I don't wish to be unkind, but does anyone still believe that by fiddling around with double exposures Man Ray revealed the inner Reality of Kiki of Montparnasse?

Because they are vague and ultimately ungraspable, metaphysical Realities are easy. All artists have to do is claim that they have unveiled this or that facet of the Real, and we go along with the claim or we don't, for reasons that have less to do with art than with our emotional needs. By contrast, appearances are difficult, because any depiction is an interpretation, which the artist offers to us to be interpreted further, and the end is never in sight. In the realm of appearances — the ordinary world we all inhabit — meaning is always up for grabs. A scrupulous realist, Remfry has no use for those devices, those clichés, which allow us to suspend interpretation and settle comfortably into a certitude.

For example, in one of Remfry's club scenes you might run across a young man with a bare torso, in a black leather vest and a black leather cap — a tough-guy outfit with a hint of sexual threat. His features are strong and yet, in Remfry's rendering, they have a degree of delicacy. So, what have we

here? A piece of rough trade or a sensitive young man who, for reasons that might turn out to be not all that inscrutable, has chosen to play a certain part? It is entirely up to you to decide, and, as you do, bear in mind that there is no reason on earth — as opposed to the heaven of immediately decipherable clichés — that a piece of rough trade can't have delicate features. Remember, too, that gay and straight are not absolutes. They appear on continuum, and at every point you may well find a guy in black leather.

From the sophistication of Remfry's pictorial technique flows a sophistication about the people he pictures. Thus he lets them be in his art what all of us are in life: conundrums. Sexuality, character, social status: none of these is uncomplicated, and sophistication does not consist in reducing complexity to simplicity. Rather, it consists in knowing what is possible for people to be, and in realizing that, within the ample space of possibility, truth is always ambiguous. Nor, as Remfry suggests with his beguiling cast of characters, is there any point in yearning for simple truths. They wouldn't be satisfying. Yearn instead to be as versatile as Remfry. How can a painter be so acute about youth, at its moment of ultimate stylishness, and about older people who have learned the hard

TANGO
1999
Watercolor on Paper
60 x 20 in.

way to be skeptical about the promises of style?

Or one might wish for the casual tolerance that Remfry's people show themselves and one another, for he is not merely a realist. His realism has a utopian tinge. Even his most crowded dance floors are, in their way, ideal places where people are absolutely free to define themselves as they wish—and, just as important, with just the degree of precision that suits them. Does a young female wear the dress she does because its plainness can be read as girlish or because its clinginess reveals her womanly form? Nothing in her face or posture or the way her hand rests on her partner's shoulder makes it easy to settle this question, which may be unanswerable. These two alternatives, after all, are not incompatible.

And what about the middle-aged man in jacket and bow tie? Is he abashed by his excess weight and determined to ignore it or does he sport it as an emblem of appetites he wants—or expects—other dancers to satisfy? I think of a stock character, the lustful buffoon. Another figure might bring to mind the secretly passionate wallflower or the *grande dame* made imperious by her disappointments. But not one of these labels sticks. Remfry doesn't deal in stereotypes. Amazingly, no one in his pictures—not one of the hundreds of people he has painted—is anything less than a fully particular person.

I don't deny, of course, that we all draw on a common pool of possibilities for dress and attitude. When a cliché appears in Remfry's art—that black leather vest, for example, or a man's evening clothes on a girl with short hair—we read it as the choice of the person depicted, not the artist's imposition. Remfry sees how tempting it is to identify oneself with styles and stereotypes. He also sees that the identification can never be perfect. As social creatures, we are shaped by others' expectations, including the one that encourages us to realize our individualities. Even as we accept readymade definitions of ourselves, we try to step outside them. Remfry shows how people do that: half-consciously, for the most part, and often with the tacit support of those around them. Individuality, it turns out, is a collaborative project.

Nothing in Remfry's art is more urban than the transience of his subjects. People appear once and then are gone forever. Among the few exceptions is a pair of women, Lindy and Jessica.

During 1987, the artist pictured these friends of
his often, first in ink sketches, then in paintings.
Though most of the latter are in his usual medium,
watercolor, these subjects prompted him to make
one of his rare paintings in oils. Remfry, it seems,
couldn't get enough of Lindy and Jessica. One
sees the fascination. Both have strong, immediately
recognizable features. Moreover, they take such
pleasure in dramatizing the postures of the dance
— and in being together.

The obvious inference is that Lindy and
Jessica are gay and smitten with one another. That
may well be the case. Just because an inference
is obvious doesn't mean that it is wrong. But, as
usual, Remfry's realism gives art all the richness —
which is to say, all the ambiguity — of life. Refusing
to supply cues of the simple kind that make
interpretation easy, Remfry leaves us free to sup-
pose that Lindy and Jessica aren't gay. They like
to dance together because they have found, as
women often do, that men are boring partners.
Dancing with women is more amusing, and if this
preference has sexual implications — as inevitably
it must — well, so what?

I like the interpretation that sees Lindy
and Jessica as uninhibited straight women with
a great sense of fun, because it makes the two
women more available to my imagination. But I
don't insist that I am right. To paraphrase Joseph
Conrad, I am not one of the happy ones who
believe something is true just because it suits
them. Remfry proposes that we seek a different,
less narcissistic sort of happiness: the delight
to be had by stepping beyond one's convenient
assumptions, into the public realm where the
meaning of things is being questioned, revised,
remade. This, as I've been suggesting, is the realm
of Remfry's art. We can't be part of it literally, but
that is all right, because nothing is literal here.

All is figurative, by which I mean not only that
Remfry is a painter of figures. More than that, his
figures invite us to figure them out. Each of his
people is like an intricate figure of speech, waiting
to be interpreted. As interpretation proceeds, you
eventually realize that all your tastes and interests,
your beliefs and inclinations, are becoming visible.
An image of yourself has emerged. Interpretation
has become self-interpretation, and — not literally
but figuratively — you have arrived at the center of
the scene you've been trying to understand.

DANCERS (details)

Alanna Heiss

Alanna Heiss Is your work portraiture?

David Remfry I don't think of it as portraiture.
I think of it simply as painting. When Ray Charles
was asked if he was a blues singer, he replied,
"No, but I am a singer who is able to sing the blues."
I am not a portrait painter, but a painter able to
paint portraits.

When I am working on a large painting, I
may draw a figure many times and combine it with
other figures and information I have gathered
to make a more complex painting, which I don't
regard as portraiture. The work may originate
in a situation I've observed at a club or a party or
dance, which becomes the germ of an idea for a
large work. It may be the mood or the atmosphere
or the way the people are moving that excites that
first feeling. I try to recreate the *feeling*, not the
literal reality.

AH Do you always paint people? (Why?)

DR I'm fascinated by the human predicament.
I'm obsessed with people, with us, how we behave
together. The things that link us, what we do
together, what we do after hours, after a drink or
two at clubs, at bars and at parties. How we
embrace as we dance, how we 'distract ourselves'
as Francis Bacon put it. I love observing all this
and recording 'it' in a painting. In the process, I
hope to discover something of what we are.

AH You call the large works 'paintings' but
they are really great big watercolors. What is your
definition of painting?

DR I use the same gestures in watercolor as I use
when working in oil. I use a large brush, loaded
with pigment, over a flat surface; I call that painting.
Works produced by this means are paintings no less
so than fresco, encaustic, oil, tempera or the rest.

Watercolor presents interesting challenges.
It can be pale and translucent, thinly pigmented
or the pigment can be dense and saturated
into the paper, far from the polite little interiors
or landscapes which are often thought to be the
province of watercolor.

AH Do you use models?

DR Models are an essential part of the way
I work. I prefer not to use professional models,
but people who possess some quality that suits
my painting.

New York, which I've always loved and
became my home six years ago, is chokingly rich
in subject matter. Quentin Crisp said all the
people are beautiful in New York. I'd love to
include it all, but obviously it would be impossible, so editing out material or possibilities is
as much a part of the job as gathering it.

Much of my work is around the subject of
people dancing, so this is what I ask them to do
in the studio. They chew up the floor with their
heels whilst I stand and observe and draw.

AH How fast or slow do you work?

DR I do something every day. The painting
is relatively fast. I may paint a full-length figure
in a day, sometimes more. But the information
gathering, the studies, the juggling, juxtaposition-
ing, the accumulation of material for a painting
can take months or years.

29

Plates

DANCERS
Undated
Watercolor on Paper
40 x 27 in.

32

DANCERS
1986
Watercolor on Paper
42¼ x 29¾ in.

DANCERS
1986
Watercolor on Paper
37½ x 31½ in.

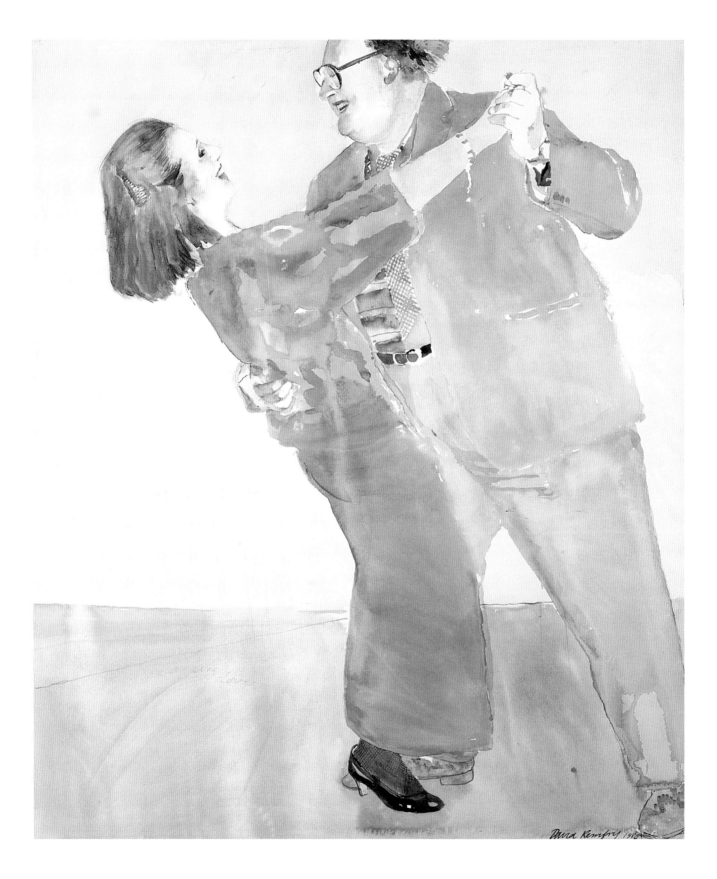

DANCERS
Undated
Watercolor on Paper
47¾ x 24½ in.

DANCERS
Undated
Graphite on Paper
27¼ x 20¼ in.

DANCERS
Undated
Watercolor on Paper
12½ x 9¼ in.

DANCERS
Undated
Graphite on Paper
13¾ x 10 in.

DANCERS
1986
Watercolor on Paper
40 x 29 in.

DANCERS
1986
Watercolor on Paper
40½ x 27¼ in.

DANCERS
1985
Graphite on Paper
25½ x 19½ in.

44

DANCERS
1986
Graphite and Watercolor on Paper
33 x 27¼ in.

DANCER
Undated
Graphite and Wash on Paper
40¼ x 27¼ in.

48

DANCER
1990
Watercolor on Paper
48 x 30 in.

DANCERS
2000
Graphite on Paper
41 x 26 in.

WALK IN, DANCE OUT
1987
Graphite and Wash on Paper
42¾ x 30¼ in.

DANCERS
1986
Watercolor on Paper
42¾ x 29¾ in.

DANCERS
1986
Oil on Canvas
40½ x 31½ in.

DANCERS
1987
Graphite and Wash on Paper
40½ x 27¼ in.

DANCERS
1987
Watercolor on Paper
40½ x 27¼ in.

DANCERS
1995
Graphite on Paper
40¾ x 25¼ in.

**WALTZ ME ONCE AGAIN
AROUND THE DANCE FLOOR**
1995
Watercolor on Paper
72 x 90 in.

DANCERS
1995
Watercolor on Paper
60 x 25½ in.

DANCERS
1995
Watercolor on Paper (Two panels)
52¼ x 24 in.

DANCERS (study)
1987
Graphite on Paper
8¼ x 5¼ in.

DANCERS
Undated
Oil on Canvas
48 x 44 in.

DANCERS
1987
Graphite on Paper
40 x 27 in.

DANCERS
1987
Watercolor on Paper
47¾ x 30⅛ in.

DANCERS (study)
1987
Graphite on Paper
8¼ x 5¼ in.

DANCERS
1987
Watercolor on Paper
47¾ x 30 in.

DANCERS
Undated
Watercolor on Paper
47¼ x 23¾ in.

DANCERS
1987
Oil on Canvas
44 x 40 in.

SWING
1998
Watercolor on Paper (Three panels)
60 x 120 in.

DANCERS
2001
Graphite and Wash on Paper
60 x 40 in.

DANCERS
2001
Graphite and Wash on Paper
48 x 31½ in.

DANCERS
1990
Watercolor on Paper
47¾ x 24¼ in.

DANCERS
1991
Watercolor on Paper
40½ x 27¼ in.

DANCERS
1991
Watercolor on Paper
40¼ x 27¼ in.

DANCERS
1991
Watercolor on Paper
47¾ x 25 in.

DANCERS
1986
Watercolor on Paper
40 x 29 in.

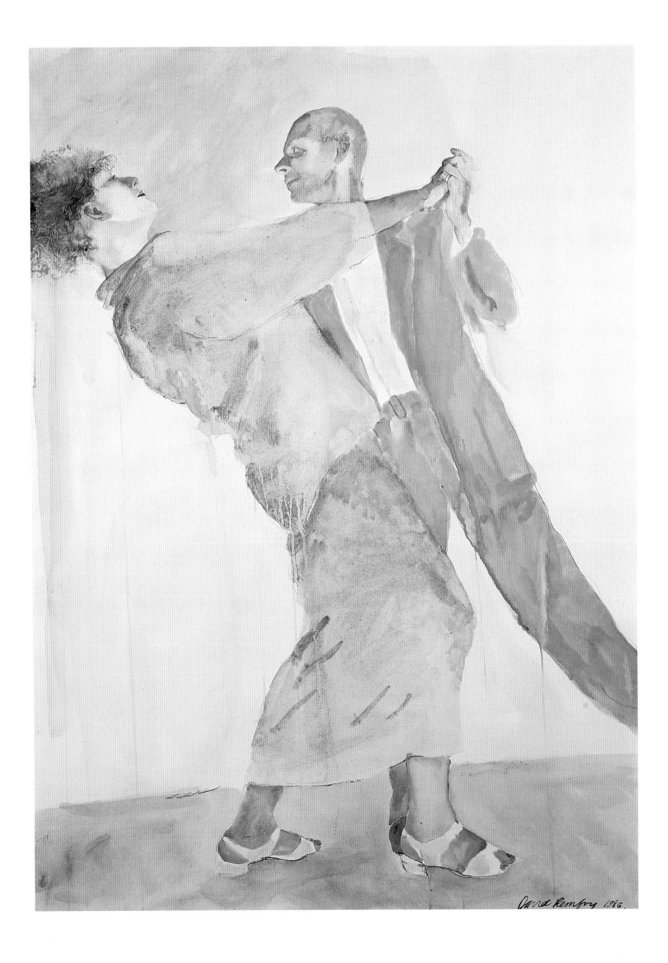

QUICK QUICK – SLOW SLOW
1990
Graphite on Paper
40½ x 27¼ in.

David Rembry 1990.

DANCERS
Undated
Watercolor on Paper
47¾ x 30 in.

DANCERS
Undated
Watercolor on Paper
48 x 29¾ in.

DANCERS
1988
Watercolor on Paper
Triptych
Left panel 48 x 35½ in.
Middle panel 48 x 35½ in.
Right panel 48 x 30 in.

UNTITLED STUDY
2000
Graphite and Wash on Paper
20¼ x 13¼ in.

UNTITLED STUDY
2000
Graphite and Wash on Paper
20¼ x 13¼ in.

84

DANCER
Undated
Graphite and Wash on Paper
40¾ x 26 in.

UNTITLED STUDY
2000
Graphite and Wash on Paper
20¼ x 13¼ in.

LATIN CLUB III
2000
Watercolor on Paper
60 x 40 in.

DANCERS
Undated
Watercolor on Paper
40¼ x 27¼ in.

DANCERS
1999/2000
Watercolor on Paper (Two panels)
40 x 120 in.

CLUB ELITE
1997
Watercolor on Paper
47 x 40 in.

PARTY
1997
Watercolor on Paper
60 x 40 in.

DANCERS
1987
Graphite and Wash on Paper
40¼ x 27¼ in.

DANCERS
1988
Watercolor on Paper
48 x 30 in.

FIVE WOMEN
2000
Watercolor on Paper (Two panels)
60 x 80 in.

DANCERS
2000
Watercolor on Paper (Two panels)
60 x 80 in.

O BODY SWAYED TO MUSIC
1999
Watercolor on Paper (Two panels)
60 x 80 in.

A LITTLE NIGHT MUSIC
Undated
Watercolor on Paper
40 x 60 in.

UNTITLED STUDY
2001
Graphite and Wash on Paper
20¼ x 13¼ in.

UNTITLED STUDY
2001
Graphite and Wash on Paper
20¼ x 13¼ in.

UNTITLED STUDY
2000
Graphite and Wash on Paper
20¼ x 13¼ in.

DANCERS
2001
Watercolor on Paper (Two panels)
40 x 100 in.

DANCERS
Undated
Watercolor on Paper
40¼ x 27½ in.

DANCERS
1994
Graphite on Paper
32 x 27¼ in.

MR. AND MRS. ARNOLD ROSS
1995
Watercolor on Paper
50 x 22 in.

DANCERS
1990
Watercolor on Paper
40½ x 27¼ in.

DANCERS
1988/9
Watercolor on Paper
40¼ x 27¼ in.

DANCERS
1989
Watercolor on Paper
40 x 27 in.

DANCERS
1990
Graphite on Paper
40¾ x 25¼ in.

David Remfry NY 1997

DANCERS
2000
Graphite and Wash on Paper
20 x 16 in.

DANCER
1985
Graphite on Paper
40¼ x 27¼ in.

MILONGA
2002
Watercolor on Paper
60 x 40 in.

DANCERS
1991
Watercolor on Paper
48 x 30 in.

NIGHTLIFE
2001
Watercolor on Paper
40 x 100 in.

TANGO
1999
Watercolor on Paper
40½ x 26 in.

LITHOGRAPHS AND

SELECTED SKETCHBOOKS

DANCERS I
1988
Lithograph on Paper
35¾ x 24¾ in.

DANCERS II
1988
Lithograph on Paper
35¼ x 26¾ in.

DANCERS III
1988
Lithograph on Paper
35¼ x 26¾ in.

TO DANCE AND TO BE LOVED
7 November 1987
Graphite on Paper, 8¼ x 5¼ in.

DANCERS
31 Dec 1987
Graphite on Paper, 8¼ x 5¼ in.

DANCERS
February 87
Graphite on Paper, 8¼ x 5¼ in.

DANCERS
1st March 87
Graphite on Paper, 8¼ x 5¼ in.

DANCERS
February 87
Graphite on Paper, 8¼ x 5¼ in.

DANCERS
30 Dec 87
Graphite on Paper, 8¼ x 5¼ in.

DANCERS
Undated
Graphite on Paper, 8¼ x 5¼ in.

DANCERS
2nd May 1987
Graphite on Paper, 8¼ x 5¼ in.

DANCERS
17 November 1988
Watercolor on Paper
8¼ x 5¼ in.

Full Index of Paintings and Selected Bibliography

INDEX OF DAVID REMFRY PAINTINGS

p. 80 **DANCERS**
(Tea Dance, Hammersmith
Town Hall, London)
Undated
Watercolor on Paper
47¾ x 30 in.
121 x 76 cm.

p. 81 **DANCERS**
(Tea Dance, Hammersmith
Town Hall, London)
Undated
Watercolor on Paper
48 x 29¾ in.
122 x 75 cm.

pp. 82–3 **DANCERS**
(Tea Dance, Hammersmith
Town Hall, London)
1988
Watercolor on Paper
Triptych
Left panel 48 x 35½ in.,
121 x 90 cm.
Middle panel 48 x 35½ in.,
121 x 90 cm.
Right panel 48 x 30 in.,
121 x 76 cm.

p. 84 **UNTITLED STUDY**
LEFT 2000
Graphite and Wash on Paper
20¼ x 13¼ in.
52 x 34 cm.

p. 84 **UNTITLED STUDY**
RIGHT 2000
Graphite and Wash on Paper
20¼ x 13¼ in.
52 x 34 cm.

p. 85 **THE WAY THE MEN DANCE**
2002
Watercolor on Paper
60 x 40 in.
153 x 102 cm.

p. 86 **DANCER**
LEFT (Alie Amonoo)
Undated
Graphite and Wash on Paper
40¾ x 26 in.
103 x 66 cm.

p. 86 **UNTITLED STUDY**
RIGHT 2000
Graphite and Wash on Paper
20¼ x 13¼ in.
52 x 34 cm.

p. 87 **LATIN CLUB III**
2000
Watercolor on Paper
60 x 40 in.
153 x 102 cm.
Private Collection

p. 88 **DANCERS**
Undated
Watercolor on Paper
40¼ x 27¼ in.
102 x 69 cm.

p. 89 **SWING DANCE I**
2001
Watercolor on Paper
60 x 40 in.
153 x 102 cm.
Courtesy of Neuhoff Gallery, NY

pp. 90–1 **DANCERS**
1999/2000
Watercolor on Paper (Two panels)
40 x 120 in.
102 x 305 cm.

p. 92 **CLUB ELITE**
1997
Watercolor on Paper
47 x 40 in.
120 x 102 cm.
Collection of Mr. and Mrs.
Charles Kiernan, U.S.A.
Courtesy of Jeanne Frank, NY

p. 93 **PARTY**
1997
Watercolor on Paper
60 x 40 in.
153 x 102 cm.
Collection of Barbara
Michel, U.S.A.
Courtesy of Elaine Baker
Gallery, FL

p. 94 **DANCERS**
(Katherine Graham and Truman
Capote, Black and White Ball;
from a newspaper photograph)
1987
Graphite and Wash on Paper
40¼ x 27¼ in.
102 x 69 cm.

p. 95 **DANCERS**
(Roseland Ballroom,
New York City)
1988
Watercolor on Paper
48 x 30 in.
121 x 76 cm.

p. 96 **FIVE WOMEN**
2000
Watercolor on Paper (Two panels)
60 x 80 in.
155 x 203 cm.
Private Collection, U.S.A.
Courtesy of Neuhoff Gallery, NY

p. 97 **DANCERS**
(Three Women)
2000
Watercolor on Paper (Two panels)
60 x 80 in.
155 x 203 cm.

p. 98 **O BODY SWAYED TO MUSIC**
1999
Watercolor on Paper (Two panels)
60 x 80 in.
155 x 203 cm.
Collection of Bob and
Sonny Barnett, U.S.A.
Courtesy of Elaine Baker
Gallery, FL

p. 99 **A LITTLE NIGHT MUSIC**
Undated
Watercolor on Paper
40 x 60 in.
102 x 152 cm.

p. 100 **UNTITLED STUDY**
LEFT 2001
Graphite and Wash on Paper
20¼ x 13¼ in.
52 x 34 cm.

p. 100 **UNTITLED STUDY**
RIGHT 2001
Graphite and Wash on Paper
20¼ x 13¼ in.
52 x 34 cm.

p. 101 **UNTITLED STUDY**
2000
Graphite and Wash on Paper
20¼ x 13¼ in.
52 x 34 cm.

pp. 102–3 **DANCERS**
Untitled
2001
Watercolor on Paper (Two panels)
40 x 100 in.
102 x 254 cm.

p. 104 **DANCERS**
Undated
Watercolor on Paper
40¼ x 27½ in.
102 x 69 cm.

p. 105 **DANCERS**
1991
Oil on Canvas
52 x 40 in.
132 x 102 cm.

p. 106 **DANCERS**
(Mr. and Mrs. Arnold Ross)
1994
Graphite on Paper
32 x 27¼ in.
81 x 69 cm.

p. 107 **MR. AND MRS.**
ARNOLD ROSS
1995
Watercolor on Paper
50 x 22 in.
127 x 56 cm.
Collection of Mr. and Mrs.
Arnold Ross, NY

SOLO EXHIBITIONS

DAVID REMFRY was born in
Worthing on the south coast of
England in 1942. In 1949 his family
moved to Kingston upon Hull, East
Yorkshire. He studied at Hull College
of Art from 1959–1964 when he
moved to London and in 1995 he
moved to New York. Remfry was
elected a member of the Royal
Watercolour Society in 1987, was
made a Fellow of the Royal Society
of the Arts in 1989 and in 2001
was awarded the M.B.E. for services
to British Art in America by Her
Majesty Queen Elizabeth II.

2005 **Fitzwilliam Museum**
Cambridge, England

2003 **Neuhoff Gallery**
New York City

2002 **Boca Raton Museum of Art**
Boca Raton, Florida

Elaine Baker Gallery
Boca Raton, Florida

P.S. 1 Contemporary Art Center
New York City
(Museum of Modern Art affiliate)

2001 **Neuhoff Gallery**
New York City

1999 **Boca Raton Museum of Art**
Boca Raton, Florida

Elaine Baker Gallery
Boca Raton, Florida

Neuhoff Gallery
New York City

1997 **Lipworth International Art**
Fort Lauderdale, Florida

Mercury Gallery
London

1996 **Bohun Gallery**
Henley-On-Thames, England

Tatistcheff Gallery
New York City

1995 **Portal Gallery**
Bremen, Germany

Royal Society of Arts
London

1994 **Mercury Gallery**
London

Old Fire Engine House
Ely, England

1993 **Bohun Gallery**
Henley-On-Thames, England

Lipworth International Art
Boca Raton, Florida

Portal Gallery
Bremen, Germany

1992 **Lipworth International Art**
Fort Lauderdale, Florida

Mercury Gallery
London

National Portrait Gallery
London

Old Fire Engine House
Ely, England

1991 **Bohun Gallery**
Henley-On-Thames, England

1990 **Mercury Gallery**
London

Old Fire Engine House
Ely, England

Zack Schuster Gallery
Fort Lauderdale, Florida

1988 **Mercury Gallery**
London, England

Zack Schuster Gallery
Fort Lauderdale, Florida

1987 **Ankrum Gallery**
Los Angeles

Bohun Gallery
Henley-On-Thames, England

1986 **Mercury Gallery**
London

Old Fire Engine House
Ely, England

Zack Schuster Gallery
Fort Lauderdale, Florida

1985 **Ankrum Gallery**
Los Angeles

Bohun Gallery
Henley-On-Thames, England

1984 **Mercury Gallery**
London

1983 **Ankrum Gallery**
Los Angeles

Bohun Gallery
Henley-On-Thames, England

Galerie de Beerenburght
Eck en Wiel, Holland

Mercury Gallery
Edinburgh Scotland

Old Fire Engine House
Ely, England

1982 **Galerie de Beerenburght**
Eck en Wiel, Holland

Mercury Gallery
London

1981 **Ankrum Gallery**
Los Angeles

Bohun Gallery
Henley-On-Thames, England

Middlesbrough Art Gallery
Middlesbrough, England

Old Fire Engine House
Ely, England

1980 **Ankrum Gallery**
Los Angeles

Galerie de Beerenburght
Eck en Wiel, Holland

Mercury Gallery
London

1979 **Old Fire Engine House**
Ely, England

1978 **Mercury Gallery**
London

Bohun Gallery
Henley-On-Thames, England

Galerie de Beerenburght
Eck en Wiel, Holland

1977 **Old Fire Engine House**
Ely, England

1976 **Folkstone Art Gallery**
Kent, England

1975 **Ferens Municipal Gallery**
Kingston upon Hull, England

Old Fire Engine House
Ely, England

1974 **Editions Graphiques**
London

1973 **New Grafton Gallery**
London

WORK IN
PUBLIC COLLECTIONS

Boca Raton Museum of Art
Florida

British Museum
London

Butler Institute of Art
Youngstown, OH

Contemporary Art Society
London

Fitzwilliam Museum
Cambridge, England

Middlesbrough Art Gallery
England

Minnesota Museum of American Art
Saint Paul

National Portrait Gallery
London

New Orleans Museum of Art

Museo Rayo
Roldanillo, Colombia

Swarthmore College
Swarthmore, Pennsylvania

The Royal Collection
Windsor, England

Victoria and Albert Museum
London

Whitworth Art Gallery
Manchester, England

SELECTED BIBLIOGRAPHY

BOOKS, BROCHURES AND CATALOGUES

Book, (In hardcover and soft-back) David Remfry Dancers, David Remfry exhibition at the Boca Raton Museum of Art, Florida, November 12, 2002–January 12, 2003, touring to the Fitzwilliam Museum, Cambridge, England in 2005. Essays by Edward Lucie-Smith, 'David Remfry Dancers', Dore Ashton 'The Dance' and Carter Ratcliff 'The Meaning of the Dance, the Dance of Meaning'.

Exhibition brochure, David Remfry at P.S.1 Contemporary Arts Center, New York City, Museum of Modern Art Affiliate, October 20, 2001–January 19, 2002. David Remfry interviewed by Alanna Heiss.

Exhibition catalogue, David Remfry at Neuhoff Gallery, New York City, October 11–November 8, 2001. Essay by Robert C. Morgan. 'Lunar Creatures: New Watercolors by David Remfry.'

Exhibition catalogue, David Remfry at Neuhoff Gallery, New York City, October 20–December 4, 1999. Essay by Phyllis Tuchman, 'David Remfry, Sleepless City.'

Exhibition catalogue, David Remfry at the Boca Raton Museum of Art, Florida, March 26–May 9, 1999. Essay by George S. Bolge, 'David Remfry, Personages.'

Festival catalogue, David Remfry, featured artist at The Festival Gallery as part of the Henley Festival, Henley on Thames, England, July 10–13, 1996. Essay by William Packer, 'David Remfry at Henley.'

Exhibition catalogue, David Remfry at Tatistcheff & Company, New York City, January 30–February 24, 1996. 'David Remfry, Gotham Nights.'

Exhibition catalogue, David Remfry at Margaret Lipworth International Art, Boca Raton, Florida. December 2, 1993–January 4, 1994. 'David Remfry, What Makes Us Tick?'

Exhibition brochure, David Remfry, Middlesbrough Art Gallery, May 30–June 20, 1981.

Exhibition catalogue, David Remfry at Folkstone Art Gallery, Kent, England, March 12–April 18, 1976. Foreword by Marina Vaizey.

Exhibition brochure, David Remfry, Ferens Art Gallery, December 13, 1974–January 11, 1975.

Exhibition catalogue, David Remfry, Editions Graphiques Gallery, 1974. Essay by Victor Arwas.

ARTICLES AND REVIEWS IN THE PRESS

2002   Gerrit Henry, "David Remfry at Neuhoff and P.S.1," Art in America, May

William Packer, "Enjoys a return to the Royal Academy Summer Show," Financial Times, July 6/7, England

2001   Nicholas Wapshott, "A New York state of mind," The Times, October 24, England

Steve Regan, "An artist from over here who's famous over there," Hull Daily Mail, January 17, England

Neala Schwartzberg, "Experience Contemporary Art at its Best," LIEYE.com, Autumn

2000   Courtney Powers Curtiss, "David Remfry, Figuratively Speaking," Florida Design Magazine Volume 10, Number 2

1999   Candice Russell, "Cresting Watercolor," City Link, Palm Beach, Florida, April 21

"What's Hot Around Town: Watercolor Magic," The Palm Beach Post, April 2

Deborah K. Dietsch, "Color and Curls," Sun-Sentinel, Florida, April 8

Gary Schwan, "Remfry's watercolors offer compelling mix," Palm Beach Post, April 2

Skip Sheffield, "Remfry at Boca Museum of Art," Boca Raton News, April 26

Skip Sheffield, "Boca Museum of Art: 3 New Shows," Boca Raton News, March 24

Eloise David-Chopin, "A Kaleidoscope of Movement," Palm Beach Illustrated, March

Susan Hartenstein, "From The Artist Studio," Rockwave.com, October

1998   "New York, artists in Chelsea," GQ, May, Japan

Richard Dorment, "At last the RA gets it right," artcriticlondon.com, Summer

1997   Anthony J. Lester, "Contemporary British Artists: A Personal Choice," Antique Collecting, October, England

"Where Quality Matters, David Remfry in Ambit Magazine," Ham & High, October 31, England

1996   Felicity Owen, "Taken by Surprise," The Spectator, July 27, England

Camilla Shelley, "Featuring David Remfry," Henley Observer, July, England

1995   "David Remfry at Portal Gallery," Sonnabend, March 18, Bremen, Germany

"David Remfry," Bremer Anzeiger, March 18, Bremen, Germany

1994   "David Remfry at Mercury Gallery," Boardroom Magazine, August, England

"Way Ahead," Daily Express, July 16, London

Robin Dutt, "David Remfry at Mercury Gallery," What's On In London, July, England

"David Remfry, Mercury Gallery," Apollo Magazine, July, England

William Packer, "Ambitions Beyond the Simple Portrait," Financial Times, July 2, England

"David Remfry at Mercury Gallery," Royal Society for the Arts Journal, June, England

Felicity Owen, "Independent Spirits," Country Life Magazine, May 12, England

1993   "David Remfry at Bohun Gallery," Art Review, November, England

"David Remfry at Bohun Gallery," House and Gardens, October, England

"Around the Galleries," Henley Standard, October 29, England

"David Remfry," Turbo First, October, England

"The Hunting/Observer Art Prizes," Watercolors, Drawings and Prints, Spring, England

"David Remfry at Bohun Gallery," Art Review, May, England

"David Remfry, Hunting/Observer Art Prize," The Observer Magazine, January 31, England

1992   Fionnula McHugh, "Changing Faces," Telegraph Magazine, May, England

Anthony J. Lester, "Today's Talents," *Watercolours Drawings and Prints Magazine*, April, England

1991 Sheridan Morley, "Answer on a postcard," *The Independent*, June 7, England

Jane Norrie, "David Remfry at Bohun Gallery," *Arts Review,* May 3, England

Jane Norrie, "David Remfry at Bohun Gallery," *Arts Review,* April 19, England

1990 William Packer, "Mainly homegrown talent," *Financial Times*, June 5, England

1989 Jennifer Allen, "Joan Rivers," *Architectural Digest,* February

1988 Florence Gould, "David Remfry, A Romantic Era Revisited," *The News*, Miami, June 19

William Packer, "David Remfry," *Financial Times*, June 7, England

"David Remfry," *Miami Herald,* February

Lori Campbell, "Roaring Twenties redux," *The News*, Miami, January 18

"Zack Schuster Gallery Presents David Remfry Showing," *Future Florida*, January 19

1987 Jane Norrie, "David Remfry at Bohun Gallery," *Art Review*, October 23, England

1986 "David Remfry," *Hombre Magazine*, August 8, Holland

Max Wykes Joyce, "Exhibition Reviews, David Remfry," *Art and Artist,* July, England

"David Remfry," *Future Florida*, June

Millie Wolff, "David Remfry," *Palm Beach Daily News*, March 9,

"Remfry's Recent Paintings Open at Zack Schuster," *Palm Beach Daily News*, March 9

Judi Grove, "David Remfry pulled success out of his hats," *Evening Times*, March 25, England

1984 "Hat Stand," *Observer Magazine*, October 23, England

"Warts & All," *Portrait Magazine*, October, England

Terrence Mullaly, "Art," *Daily Telegraph*, October 2, England

"David Remfry at Mercury Gallery," *Arts and Artists Magazine*, September, England

"Less Familiar Waters," *Ham and High*, May 4, England

Oswell Blakeston, "London Reviews, David Remfry," *Arts Review*, April 11, England

"Getting Ahead," *Daily Telegraph,* April 24, England

Oswell Blakeston, "David Remfry," *Arts Review*, March 8, England

Tuppy Wens, "Private View," *Alpha Magazine*, England

1983 Caroline Collier, "David Remfry, Bohun Gallery," *Arts Review,* October 14, England

1982 "Portrait," *Sunday Times Magazine*, November 28, England

1981 "Artist in the picture," *Evening Gazette*, June 1, England

1980 Twee Sympathieke Britten in De Galerie, *Eugen Huis*, October, Holland

Beerenburght, "Review of show in Holland," *Eugen Huis,* November 28, Holland

Terrence Mullaly, "...before she go there, the cupboard was bare," *Daily Telegraph*, July 26, England

"Miss Jean Muir, A drawing commissioned by The Times," *The Times*, May 20, England

"Painter who sees young as witless, Mercury Gallery," *Daily Telegraph*, April 15, England

Joy Hanington, "Picture Furniture at Mercury Gallery," *Homes and Gardens*, February, England

1978 "Images of Chilhood, Bohun Gallery," *Sunday Times*, October 15, England

Oswell Blakeston, "David Remfry, Mercury Gallery," October 3, *Arts Review,* England

Janet Daley, "New Figuration," *Arts Review,* August 10, England

Jane Daley, "New Figuration," *Arts Review,* June 9, England

1977 Srdja Djukanovic, "The London Season," *Daily Telegraph*, May 23, England

1976 "David Remfry, Portraits," *South London Press*, November 26, England

New Grafton Gallery Portraits, *The Times,* March 18, England

1975 W.E. Johnson, "Figure it all out yourself," *Middlesbrough Evening Gazette*, July 15, England

Richard Walker, "Artists of Today and Tomorrow," *Arts Review,* July 25, England

"Review of New Grafton Gallery exhibition," *Daily Mail*, July 13, England

Pru Clark, "Hull Ferens Exhibition is Devoted to the Work of Four Young Artists," *Daily Mail,* February 19, England

1974 "Don't just sit there — POSE!," *Evening Standard,* November 15, England

142

George S. Bolge
Executive Director

Valerie Johnson
Assistant to the Executive Director

Curatorial

Wendy M. Blazier
Senior Curator

David Carone
Registrar

Jeanne Mautoni
Curatorial Assistant

Education

Richard Frank
Curator of Education

Katherine Darr
Associate Education Curator

Maria Brueggeman
Curatorial Assistant

Sarah Gubin
Chairperson Docent Council (V)

Rosalind Yewdell
School Tour Coordinator (V)

Betty & Marvin Koenig
Art Reference Librarians (V)

Finance

Carolyn J. Benham
Director of Finance & Human Resources

Vivienne Wilson
Accountant

Amy Cassaro
Receptionist

Barbara Mango
Museum Shop Manager

Teoman Algur
Facility Manager

Robin Archible
Facility Manager

Connie Bowers
Office Assistant (V)

Marketing

Kae Jonsons
Director of Marketing

Julie Kaminski
Public Relations Manager

Isabella Eckart
Membership/Group Sales Coordinator

Marcia Nathans
Membership Coordinator

Carmie Pepe
Office Assistant (V)

School

Rebecca Sanders
Art School Administrator

Lynn Nance
Receptionist/Office Assistant

William McConnell
Art School Building & Grounds Superintendent

(V) denotes volunteer

The Boca Raton Museum of Art wishes to express its thanks to the following sources of photographs and illustrations.

PHOTOGRAPHS

Unless otherwise credited, all photographs are courtesy of David Remfry. All photographs of Remfry paintings are by Beth Phillips, New York City, and Prudence Cumming, London.

Photograph of Edward Lucie-Smith and David Remfry at the Hotel Chelsea, January 17, 2002. ©Rita Barros, New York City.

ILLUSTRATIONS

Sitting Woman with Her Right Leg Bent, 1917, Watercolor, Gouache and Charcoal on Paper, by Egon Schiele (1890–1918): Phillips, The International Fine Art Auctioneers, UK/Bridgeman Art Library.

Emilie Floge, 1902, Oil on Canvas, by Gustav Klimt (1862–1918): Historisches Museum der Stadt, Vienna, Austria/Bridgeman Art Library.

Harris Theatre, New York, 1940, Watercolor on Paper, by Reginald Marsh (1898–1954): Museum of the City of New York, USA/Bridgeman Art Library. ©2002 Estate of Reginald Marsh/Art Students League, New York/Artists Rights Society (ARS), New York.

Izzy Ort's, 1955, Watercolor and Pencil on Paper, by Edward Burra (1905–1976): Scottish National Gallery of Modern Art, Edinburgh, UK/Bridgeman Art Library. © The estate of Edward Burra.

Study for All Night Long, 1964, Oil on Canvas, by Michael Andrews (1928–1995): Arts Council Collection, Hayward Gallery, London, UK/Bridgeman Art Library. ©June Andrews.

Palm Beach County Florida
THE BEST OF EVERYTHING.
A TOURIST DEVELOPMENT COUNCIL FUNDED PROJECT

Florida Department of State
Katherine Harris
Secretary of State
Florida Arts Council
Division of Cultural Affairs

This program is sponsored
in part by the State of Florida,
Florida Department of State,
Division of Cultural Affairs, and
the Florida Arts Council